Raha
Celestial Healing

*The Light
Continues to Shine.*

C. S. Stacey 2017

Carol Anne Stacey

Rahanni Publishing
Maldon Essex
CM9 5DA

First published
by Rahanni Publishing April 2017

ISBN: 978-0-9567604-1-8

Cover Design & Type Setting
by Richard Avey of Hampshire U.K.

Printed in Peterborough U.K.
By Book Printing U.K.
www.bookprintinguk.com

Acknowledgements

First I wish to acknowledge the dedication to Rahanni by Neshla Avey my beautiful Teacher in Hampshire and who is now the 'Founder Elect' and will take Rahanni forward for me in the future, when it is time for me to 'go home'. Her support, love and integrity is second to none and I thank Neshla from deep within my heart for accepting Rahanni into her life, as she continues to help students on their spiritual journey. www.neshlaavey.com

I wish to thank also Margaret Cooke my dear friend from Mersea Island Essex who has supported me in every way, offering healing to me when I have been low. She is an amazing Teacher of Rahanni and Ascension workshops, but don't take my word for it – give Margaret a call. www.magentarahannicelestialhealing.com

I wish to thank all of the Guardians of Rahanni all over the world that have offered to be a support system for all Practitioners, helping them with their amazing journey.

I thank Steve Tsoi who has helped me to relax and remain calm when creating healing and meditation CDs from his studio in Great Totham Essex. www.recordingexperiences.co.uk

I thank also Mike Rowland for composing the beautiful music for Rahanni 'Of one Heart' this lovely CD has touched the hearts of many people all over the world.

Dedication

I dedicate this book to the beautiful Guides, Angels and Ascended Masters that have shown the most amazing trust in me over my life-time, especially the past 15 years. Having the knowledge that I would eventually be able to take Rahanni forward to help humanity have a change in consciousness, by opening their heart centres with the help of this beautiful healing Light.

I also dedicate this 3rd and final book to my 4 beautiful daughters, Michele, Julie, Su and Jo you have always had an open heart and have offered healing in your way, just by being in someone's life. I am so proud of you all. To my husband Barrie, that has had to adapt to the 'new' me and I guess it hasn't been easy for you, especially when Guides and Ascended Masters turn up in your bedroom late at night. That is enough to freak anyone out, but you have taken this all in your stride, so thank you for supporting me on my amazing journey; without your love and support it would have been more challenging.

I am truly blessed to have such an amazing family, not forgetting the 16 Grandchildren [7 Great Grandchildren] too numerous to mention, but they will know who they are.

Contents

Introduction

After 15 years of working with Rahanni Celestial Healing [a.k.a. Rahanni] my beautiful Guides and Angels felt it was time to write an up-date on Rahanni, how it has progressed and importantly how it has brought healing and comfort to many people over these past 15 years.

Some of the clients become so well they ask if they can be attuned to Rahanni, so they can reach out to many souls that are still suffering. When I hear this it so makes my heart sing, for I know how Rahanni has created many changes, in a positive way, not just for people, but animals also. Children seem to benefit in many ways, helping them to become calm, especially when they have been diagnosed with A.D.H.D or the parents have been told their child has a behaviour problem. It is so comforting knowing that Rahanni can possibly bring inner peace to that child and also the family, as all who live in the household will have suffered in some way with a child that is diagnosed with challenging issues.

I have also grown over the past 15 years and through the teaching of Rahanni I have also raised my vibration to a higher level of spiritual development, this has allowed me to teach ascension classes. These have been so successful, and I now have teachers in the UK that have the ability and knowledge to teach the students that are ready for their ascension.

If you are not sure what I am referring to, all will be revealed inside this book. I will just say, that every human on this planet will have to go through their ascension at some time in their existence. Sounds intriguing doesn't it? Watch this space.

I hope this book will help in some way, maybe you have been searching for that missing link in your life; perhaps you have just found it. How wonderful to be able to reach out to those who are suffering and to know within your heart you could possibly make a difference, by offering the client a better quality of life. Even if you don't want to make a business out of Rahanni, but feel you would love to be able to help your own family and friends, this is all we ask. It isn't about the amount of people you heal it is about the quality of the healing you can offer. If we help just one person, they in turn will be able to bring the healing Light to their family just by being in the same room, for we hold within our aura the beautiful healing Light that has been offered as a gift from God/Source, therefore we can help people have a change in consciousness and open their heart centre to more Love and Compassion, this in turn will help to save this planet for future generations, offering our children a more loving environment for them to continue their journey on this planet.

Love and Blessings

Carol

Looking Back

Chapter 1

As I sit in my healing room listening to Elvis singing 'I just can't help believing' accompanied by the Royal Philharmonic Orchestra, I am aware of how music has played a big part in my life, especially growing up in the 1950s and 1960s. The title of Elvis's song certainly relates to me, for as I look back to the year 2002, the year I was presented with the beautiful gift of Rahanni, little did I know then how over the next 15 years the affect Rahanni healing would have on humanity, the benefits it would bring by receiving the healing or for those who wished to become attuned to this 5th dimensional healing Light.

Certain songs would capture the heart or uplift you – so many different emotions would flow through you. Music would lift you out of a dark place or would bring tears to your eyes when a particular sound touched your heart and you would feel the love vibration – very touching. We also now know that healing with sound and colour is just as beneficial. So, yes, 'I just can't help believing' how after 15 years Rahanni has gathered momentum and is now in 24 countries – Wow! And it all started in my little 2 up 2 down house in Maldon Essex. How truly humbled and privileged I feel every day at the amount of trust my beautiful Guides and Angels have in me, to bring forward this amazing gift from God/Source.

As I continue to look back it isn't just about how humanity and animals have benefitted from the healing of Rahanni but how you grow within yourself especially after the attunement to this

5th dimensional healing Light.

I remember, back in 2002 I was at that time very dedicated with the healing modalities of Reiki and Reflexology. I had always been connected to my spiritual side from a very early age, as my dear Dad had been a healer. Unfortunately he passed to spirit age 26 with heart disease; I was only 2 years old but I remember my dear Dad as though it was yesterday. I do believe he lived long enough to help me on my spiritual journey, and I know and feel his presence even now albeit 71 years ago he passed. The love we hold in our hearts keeps us connected to our loved ones in spirit.

I have over the years, like many other people, been through many difficult and challenging situations, and if you wish to read my life story and how Rahanni came to me, this is all in my previous book 'Rahanni Celestial Healing – Embracing the Light'. I won't be going into details about these experiences in this book, for this is about progression and moving forward.

Over the years I have had a special connection with Jeshua [Jesus] for I felt he was a friend, someone to confide in and share my inner most thoughts, knowing I wouldn't be judged in any way. This has proved to be a beautiful friendship over the years as he has helped me understand the reason my soul needed to go through the many challenges – it was to get me to where I am today, with the empathy, love, compassion and understanding for all life. Nothing is wasted, everything we go through we can learn from, gain something positive from the situation. It isn't always easy, I do know that, but trust me, you will come through any trauma, as long as you have trust in the Guides and Angels and so important, trust your soul. Another important aspect of your spiritual journey is to learn to communicate with these 'Beings' of Light and love. They are but a touch away, but they cannot step forward and help, unless you ask, that is universal law, for they know we have free will, but as soon as we ask for their help, it is instant. Maybe not in the way you are expecting but you will be guided towards a person or situation that will be for your highest good and that can help you along a positive path. You just need to be open to receiving their messages.

I will endeavour to share with you spiritual information that I hope you can absorb, but that may also trigger a memory of a 'knowing' so deep inside that it resonates in your heart, bringing forward what you already know.

I had no idea I would be writing this book as I had already begun another, but for some reason I kept getting blocked until my Guide stepped forward and told me, the book I should be writing is an up-date on the first book; letting people know how Rahanni has progressed in the past 15 years and how people have benefitted from this beautiful healing Light. The Guides have been quite insistent, that this is the book I should be focusing on – so, here we are, they get their message across eventually.

Rahanni Celestial Healing [a.k.a. Rahanni] is a 5th dimensional healing modality that has never vibrated on this planet before, and the reason it wasn't brought forward any earlier is quite understandable now, as I look back. Earth was a 3rd dimensional planet, meaning the vibrations it consisted of was heavy and quite slow in comparison to now, for our planet has become 4th dimensional.

If we go back to 1987, this was the time of the Harmonic

Convergence, a time of like-minded spiritual people sending love and Light out across the planet, helping with a shift in consciousness allowing the planet to raise its vibration from the 3rd to the 4th dimension – this was accomplished and on the 21st December 2012, we became a fully anchored 4th dimensional planet – the 3rd dimension no longer exists. Anything that is still connected to 3rd dimensional vibrations will gradually be phased out. This of course will take many hundreds of years, but it will happen. A high vibration of Light cannot share the same space as a lower vibration that is universal law.

Everything on this planet has now speeded up, for how many times do we say 'there is never enough hours in the day for what we want to do.' When the planet raised it vibration to the 4th dimension it also affected humanity and everything that is living and breathing. Many people began to feel changes taking place within themselves and it was a little disconcerting for some, as they began to have a change in consciousness – the wake-up call had begun! People started to let go of so called 'friends' people they had known for years, but suddenly they no longer had anything in common with them, they found it difficult to communicate with them, and just knew they had to move on and let them go. No judgement was made, it was a recognition that those people no longer served their higher purpose. As soon as this began to happen, people becoming more aware of the changes taking place, then they began to view their present careers and therefore realised this wasn't what they wanted to do for the rest of their life- so they made changes and moved to positions where it allowed them to work in an environment where they were serving humanity, such as the caring profession, or they would go on courses to become healers, try meditation and spiritual development; they would also want to be with like-minded people, sharing a spiritual journey – this felt so right and gave them satisfaction with their new role in life. Their life had changed, their thought patterns were changing. They hadn't become religious, they had been opening up their heart centres to their natural essence, that of a spiritual being of Light, wanting answers to something they had realised they had been searching for over the past few years. At last people are finding the truth of who they really are, and what a journey this will be.

As I look back within my own journey. I can see just how much I have changed. Gone is the shy timid person with no self-confidence and lack of self-esteem, to now being a more confident [without ego] and relaxed person, able to value qualities I have within me that had been hidden for many years. All this has come from the healing I do for myself with Rahanni but also having the trust in the wonderful Guides and Angels that felt the time was right to bring Rahanni to this planet and to present me with this beautiful gift that I evidently decided, thousands of years ago that I would accept for the sake of humanity at this time of the Golden Age – an age of moving forward with an expanding heart centre and a recognition that we need to care for ourself as well as being there for others. We are just as important as the clients we care for, we have to make time to connect with nature and nature spirits, for we are of one heart – no separation.

Moving Forward

Chapter 2

Although Rahanni was presented to me as a gift in 2002 and if you have read my story you will know I had the most amazing out of body journey with Lord Melchizedek, an Ascended Master or to give him his full title – Universal Logos and Logos is an overseer of all that happens within universes. I know, this maybe a little heavy for you to take on board right now, but just let it go, it will become relevant as you become more aware of spirituality and the Higher Beings of Light that connect with us.

Just to recap from my first book, as you may not have read this yet, but I was taken out of body by Melchizedek and attuned to the Rahanni vibration and I was told a guide would come to speak with me and give me all the information of a 'new' healing modality called Rahanni. Two years later the guide arrived and after lots of questions from me to her [Kira] I had to accept this was a beautiful gift that had been offered to me to help humanity have a better quality of life and to help them have a change in consciousness. So in 2005 with all the information from Kira [my guide] I eventually began to introduce Rahanni to people of a like mind, as I thought they would be more open to receiving this information, and those that knew me would understand I hadn't lost my mind and really the proof was in the actual healing that took place on a deeper level than ever before. I was now becoming more confident with Rahanni and thought it was about time more people had the opportunity to experience this 5th dimensional healing vibration. So I set up a website and because of word of mouth, for this is the best advertising you could ever have, Rahanni has progressed beyond my wildest dreams.

I have lost count of the amount of healing sessions and teaching I have been a part of for the past 12 years and adjustments have been made over that period of time, for the guides were not quite sure how this 5th dimensional healing Light would work or be absorbed by humanity as Rahanni had never been offered to this planet before, therefore adjustments were required. We have also had other Ascended Masters and Guides step forward to work with Rahanni Practitioners and Teachers, as they wish to be a part of this amazing journey for humanity. How brilliant is that! More information on the 'new' Guides will be presented in later chapters.

So, how may you ask is Rahanni moving forward? Rahanni is now in 24 countries worldwide, and considering I do not fly or travel very far, it is testament to the popularity of Rahanni that people are more than happy to make the journey across the world to become attuned to this beautiful healing Light. It is just a joy for me when I wake up in the morning and check my emails to find another person asking to become a part of the 'Rahanni Family of Light and Love'. For this is what I feel we are, not a massive organisation with rules that are possibly outdated, but a loving family of healing Light, yes, with a Code of Ethics and everything that is required by Insurance companies; More on this later.

This will give you an idea of how Rahanni gets to other countries. I received a telephone call from a lady who asked to be attuned to Rahanni and I asked her if she wanted me to send her directions as the M25 can be very busy at times. I heard her laugh as she said 'I am coming from Bali' Oh my! Did I hear correctly, I repeated – 'Bali, I don't mean to be funny, but isn't it a long way to come just to spend a day with me' But it turned out she was visiting a friend in London and felt as she was so close it would be a lovely idea and opportunity to receive the Rahanni attunement and take it back to Bali. Another time, a lady was over here from New Zealand as I believe her husband had been offered a contract for 6 months in this country, so she thought it would be a great opportunity to come over with him as she loved to travel and see the UK. She was very connected to her spiritual side and had a crystal shop back in New Zealand, plus she offered healing at that time but wanted to see what was available here, so she viewed quite a few websites and came across my Rahanni website and felt very drawn to the energy, but wasn't sure where I lived – she found out I was only 20 minute drive away from where she was staying. She came and had a healing session with me and this led to her wanting to be attuned to Rahanni and so wanted to take it back to New Zealand. So after a few months Trish became my very first teacher in New Zealand and she hasn't looked back since. Returning home to Auckland Trish has now taught many students and I am so delighted to have Rahanni in another country. The guides work in wondrous ways to get that message across, this so touches my heart at the way it is executed with such precision by these wonderful Guides and Angels; it is beautifully done. If they want something to move forward, they will certainly place the people in the right place at the right time and help them connect with their heart centres, for their own personal spiritual development. This seems to happen so often now, it always makes me smile. The Rahanni manuals have now been translated into German, Italian and Dutch so far, I really feel this is just another move forward.

I do understand we will have sceptics, but I always say, 'Don't knock it until you have tried it'. Rahanni is very subtle, it doesn't knock you off your feet, so to speak or make you feel worse after a session, yes changes will take place and are necessary for the client's mind or body to release all that is no longer for their highest good, and this will help to bring them back into balance again. Rahanni is pure Light and Love channelled from Source/God, helping to release old ways of thinking and being to that of positive thought, love and inner peace.

One question I feel has never been answered, possibly because of lack of understanding, and that is; 'What really is healing?' So please let me offer my understanding as it has been presented to me by my guides and angels, I hope it resonates with you also.

Healing is offering a client a way of connecting to their own frequency of Light that may have possibly been lost because of life issues, trauma, fear or anxiety, all that we seem to hold on to on a daily basis. The healer, or the channel for the healing Light, for this is what we truly are, can raise our spiritual vibration to a much higher level, therefore opening areas within our 3 minds and 4 bodies, allowing us to channel through the healing vibrations from Source/God. We are just a vessel that carries a certain frequency within our energy field, which is full of spiritual knowledge and wisdom, allowing us to transfer this healing vibration known as Rahanni towards our client. As we go through the healing session, a trigger may occur where, we as the practitioner, may say something that could bring back a positive memory from a previous lifetime, but they do not necessarily accept this has happened, as it is held deep within the subconscious, but all it needed was a trigger point. The client may also pick up a vibration emanating from our aura at the time of the healing that may have a positive vibration, helping them to have a change in consciousness at a deeper level of understanding. This is why it is important when offering the healing of Rahanni, you are heart centred coming from compassion.

We, as Rahanni Practitioners and Teachers are blessed with the ability to connect with 5th dimensional vibrations, allowing us to help humanity from a higher perspective. As we become more enlightened, we hold more spiritual knowledge that we can tap into at any time, retrieving the appropriate information to pass on, helping with the gradual change in the way a client thinks and feels. It is all very subtle and gentle, but don't under-estimate the power of 5th dimensional energy.

Healing has nothing to do with the amount of books you read or workshops you attend, as you cannot find answers outside of self, all is within and all that is required will be revealed when the time is right. This is known as 'Divine Timing'. We can use books for guidance but go deep within for your inner truth that is directed from your soul/monad or I Am Presence, your beautiful connection to Source/God.

Meditation could enhance a raising of your spiritual vibration, but connecting with nature spirits and the elements of the sea will give you just as much. It is a 'feeling' a 'knowing' so deep within that you will never doubt how connected we all are to the Elemental Kingdom and Nature Spirits – just be open to their messages. When you have an open heart, it is amazing what is able to touch you and the understanding you will have on your own journey during this incarnation.

Healing isn't something you have to work hard for, in fact it is the opposite, the more relaxed you are the easier it is for you to channel through the healing Light, as nothing gets in the way. You become this beautiful channel, a conduit, you are pure and clear, that is all that is required to heal. Archangels and Ascended Masters are our teachers, they also have the 'tools' to help us with difficult situations, which is why it is important to build a relationship with these Masters of Light.

Healing isn't rocket science, it is our natural essence and who we truly are and ever will be. Every day feel the gratitude in your heart for the gift we have been given and use it wisely with Truth, Love and Compassion for our self, all of humanity, animals and plant life. One aspect of moving forward is for people to understand that when a planet raises its vibration it must have an effect on humanity; that is universal law. So all aspects of living in a 3rd dimensional way of being no longer exists, for this planet became a fully anchored 4th dimensional planet on the 21st December 2012 therefore it is having a profound effect on humanity, many changes are taking place and could be quite challenging and disconcerting for people to deal with. Because of these massive changes taking place humanity and the planet require new vibrations that work higher and on a deeper level, hence the changes with healing modalities. This brings me to a question that has been asked many times. 'What is the difference between Rahanni and Reiki?' as they are both hands-on healing. I will explain without any judgement made against Reiki or Dr. Usui, the Founder of Reiki and out of complete respect for the healing modality, for it has been an amazing healing Light since its arrival on this planet back in 1922. This is my understanding and how the guides explained to me the difference between the two therapies.

11

In 1922 Dr.Usui brought forward the healing Light known as Reiki, at this time planet Earth was 3rd dimensional, meaning the healing that was to be used for humanity had to have a vibration that was compatible with the planet's vibration and that of humanity. Dr. Usui could not have brought through a healing modality that was on a higher vibration because our physical bodies could not hold this amount of Light without it having a detrimental effect.

Reiki has been an amazing healing modality and has helped many people and will continue to do so, but this planet now is 4th dimensional, becoming fully anchored into the 4th dimension on the 21st December 2012. This means planet Earth has raised its vibration and the energy it is comprised of is lighter and finer, not heavy and dense as before.

Because the planet has raised it vibration, it has had an effect on our physical body and aura, helping it to become stronger, although lighter, therefore we can now hold higher energies within every aspect of our being. Although Rahanni is thousands of years old it was brought to this planet on the 4th August 2002, helping humanity to have a change in consciousness and to help release negativity and fear based ways of thinking to that of kindness, love and compassion. This it has managed to do beautifully, hence all the emails and testimonials I receive on a weekly basis.

Rahanni is a 5th dimensional healing modality but has the ability to connect to the 4th dimension but not the 3rd. The 3rd dimension no longer exists on this planet, as I said earlier, so therefore a higher vibration is now required for humanity. Rahanni is but one new healing Light, there will be more to follow, and who is to say that Reiki will not bring through a higher vibrational healing Light to the planet in the future, or it may be here already. Rahanni isn't any better than any other therapy, it is about progression and moving forward.

Therapists that work with 3rd dimensional frequencies will understand eventually that this has been a stepping stone on their spiritual ladder and moving to higher energies is part of their development. No judgement is made at all with regards to Reiki [I was a Reiki Master for 12 years] it is all about spiritual growth and moving forward to work with higher vibrations of healing Light. Energy isn't static, it is constantly changing, and thus we accept the need to help create these changes with our continued connection to our beautiful guides and angels. The 3rd dimension is slowly being phased out, but of course this will take hundreds of years for this to happen, and in the meantime we will all decide when it is appropriate for each one of us to release the old ways of being and move on to higher vibrations. Basically Rahanni works on a higher vibration and a deeper level therefore cutting down the healing time. Reiki will still be used as there will be many people who resonate with this healing Light.

Look how computers have changed even in the past 20 years, they were large and slow in comparison to what we use now, smaller and faster. This is growth from a planet with changing vibrations, no judgement is made – it is progression, so please do not think I am judging Reiki or any other healing modality, that is not what I do, it is fact and the understanding of the need for change in every area that we deal with here on this Earth; healing modalities are no different.

Please note:

Light with capital 'L' is the pure white Light of God/Source. light with a small 'l' is the light from the stars and the planets within the universe.

Nothing Stays the Same

Chapter 3

I do believe majority of enlightened people understand, when a planet raises its vibration everything connected to that planet must change also; it is universal law. It isn't just about the changes going on across a planet but the whole of humanity must and will change at some time. It is all to do with spiritual evolution, one is not separate from another – we are one.

A cleansing normally takes place first, either the planet will clear through earthquakes triggering off a tsunami, a change in weather conditions, or volcanic eruptions bursting forth. Everything is suddenly turned upside down and inside out. This of course can be very daunting and fearful, but even if you have a little understanding of spiritual growth and development it becomes quite a challenge to remain as calm as possible.

It isn't just the planet going through these massive shifts, it affects all of humanity at some level. Clearing spaces for new experiences, ideas and spiritual growth. As with any healing, things can get worse before they get better. Our DNA is also changing from a heavy carbon based 2 strand to a lighter and finer crystalline 12 strand DNA. These very powerful changes are necessary for the planet and humanity as the veil between the worlds is much thinner now, allowing us all to have access to more abundant and profound spiritual experiences.

Most of us understand about chakras, the energy centres flowing through our body via our central nervous system and we have known of the original 7 chakras starting at the base, this vibrates with the colour red, Sacral – orange, Solar Plexus – yellow, heart – pink/green, throat – blue, 3rd eye indigo and crown – violet and white. These chakras we have known about for a long time through our teachings, but these are also changing, because of the shifts taking place within humanity.

We could be anchoring higher chakras, depending on our level of spiritual development; let me give you an idea of the changes within this aspect of our self. There is 13 new 5th dimensional chakras available for us. You may think they are still the same but it is the intensity of the colour that has changed. The red base chakra could now be flame red, the orange sacral could be more golden but there is 2 colours that are very important for our development and that is the magenta and turquoise ray. The magenta represents strength of the feminine mind allowing women to become stronger and stand up for their beliefs. When a male absorbs this magenta ray into their aura it will help to expand the heart centre, allowing them to become more compassionate. So we all take from this ray the appropriate vibration that is required. The Turquoise ray affects us all, male and female, it represents, healing of self and a change in consciousness – so needed at this difficult time in our existence. These 2 rays of Light have been offered to humanity to help with the changes on the planet and will continue to flow here, especially every full moon and every new moon until 2028, where we should have absorbed a sufficient amount of these rays to make the changes necessary for the continuation of our planet and for that change in consciousness within every man woman and child, creating a healthier and happier environment and a beautiful world. The next 10 years will be critical and it is up to each and every one of us to take responsibility for our part in the mis-creations of humanity and vow to make the changes necessary, by recognising the need to release negativity and fear based ways of thinking, to that of love, compassion, kindness and integrity, creating a planet of love and Light for future generations.

I have seen first-hand the changes taking place in a positive way through the healing and teaching I continue to do on a weekly basis.

Another aspect of the changes taking place is that of Technology – how mind blowing is this right now! I don't know about you, but I can't keep up with all these gadgets and gizmos and apps! Oh my goodness, where will it go from here. I am sure in the future children will be born with a mobile attached to them – crazier things have happened! My Grandchildren are more informed about technology today as they have grown up with these amazing technological developments, it seems second nature to them. It is a pity that meditation isn't part of the curriculum as I am sure it would have a positive effect on these kids, helping them to relax and unwind, allowing their minds to absorb all that is for their highest good.

Something that has been a revelation is that some schools have an open mind and are allowing meditation and relaxation techniques into the classes, which is having such a positive response from students and parents alike. The children seem calmer, their behaviour is better all-round but most important the anger goes, this is so needed as we know, for too many children are diagnosed with A.D.H.D or Autism, never heard of years ago, but the pressure on children these days is immense and some just cannot cope. I am not saying meditation is a cure for these issues, but it goes a long way in helping children to relax and become calmer in the school and with home-life.

Something you may not have thought of with regards to the children being born on this planet, is that they are having difficulties adjusting to the many negative vibrations here, as they have not long arrived from the Light and their soul is struggling to adapt to these heavier dense energies on Earth, hence the way these kids are not coping. Many children become disruptive, either at home or school, they shout, as they want their voice heard, because they cannot tolerate injustice, they feel they have to have their say. At school, this doesn't go down very well as we know, they get detention, parents are possibly called to the school because of their disruptive behaviour. These poor kids are frustrated, as at a higher level of understanding they are here on Earth to change old and worn-out methods and the way we live, they are here to change these old out-dated ways, but to make these changes they need strength, will and power and maybe their mission or the career they could possibly have as an adult will be to work in Governments or Schools or places of authority where they can help these changes can take place. To do this of course they will need this energy, but unfortunately they have this amazing energy now, as a child – hence the outbursts, and have possibly been labelled with a syndrome that seems to create conflict with the Doctors – and they use the label A.D.D or A.D.H.D – Attention Deficit/Hyperactivity Disorder. The poor kids are given drugs to suppress this, so called irrational behaviour, but all it is doing is suppressing their spiritual development.

Oh I know I will be shot down in flames for even mentioning this issue, but we know it is here, we see it in the children on a daily basis. We cannot put our head in the sand and think it will change soon or go away. Things will only change when we, as adults start listening to these children, instead of talking over them and treating them as second class citizens. These children are our future and they need help now! Relaxation and meditation offered in schools is a massive step forward, I know this for a fact, for I have Practitioners that are allowed into schools to do just that – help with relaxation techniques, bringing forward gentle music and listening to them as they tone a sound or vibration that has a calming effect on their beautiful souls. The home life of the child changes also, for that calmer exterior that is shown from the child vibrates within the aura, this in turn has a positive effect on all members of the family. It is a win win situation! [Please feel free to contact me, through my website if you wish to find a Practitioner that can offer this service in schools. I will put you in touch with them.]

Meditation and relaxation is not connected to any religion as we know, in fact it is a gift for all of humanity no matter what their beliefs. It is offering a beautiful and loving way of connecting with our heart centres, helping to bring inner peace to the child. Adults would do well to try this method also, helping to bring a sense of calm and more clarity of mind, with the added bonus of having a healthier mind and body.

So many changes are taking place within our world and healing is no different. When Rahanni was first presented to me on 4th August 2002 I had no idea at that time the impact it would have on humanity. If I am honest I had no idea how I would reach out to people in other countries as I am a reluctant traveller. But my guides and angels have been working overtime, getting Rahanni recognised. They have been sending people to me from Alaska, New Zealand, U.S.A, South Africa, Australia, Canada, Switzerland, Germany Italy and the list goes on. People fly from all over to meet me, and I am truly humbled, for they have heard or received a healing of Rahanni and want to know more. Some say they connected to my website and knew straight away they had to follow this road, it was a feeling or a knowing deep inside that eventually brought them to me. I always call this 'Divine Timing' for this is just one of the wake-up calls we may receive.

Just to recap; healing modalities had to change because we are now a 4th dimensional planet, vibrating faster and moving forward at a rapid rate, so it makes sense for healing to be offered that is 5th dimensional, meaning it works on a higher vibration and a deeper level, therefore cutting down the healing time. Also the beauty of Rahanni is the change that takes place within the minds of humanity. This is so important, for the body is the reflection of the mind, so to get people to think from a different perspective and in a more positive way is paramount in any healing.

Rahanni has progressed and moved forward big time and this is shown by the amount of 'new' Ascended Masters and Guides that have stepped forward to work with all Rahanni Practitioners and Teachers. I am sure they have been waiting to see just how Rahanni would be able to work with humanity and the planet before they committed to allowing their beautiful vibration to touch the hearts of all who are connected and attuned to Rahanni. It is beautifully done, don't you think?

It is such a joy for me when I am at the computer replying to a message via email from a person having difficulties and they are asking for help and advice – before I know it a guide steps forward and away I go, channelling information that is so relevant to the person's issues, and it gets answered on a deep level of understanding, but to be honest, I just give the person the message as it was channelled through and if I was asked to speak of it the next day I wouldn't have a clue, for when you channel a guide my personality shifts to one side, allowing the guide to step forward and speak through me. It still amazes me how this works so beautifully. I feel like an 'Agony Aunt' but as long as the appropriate message is received and it helps, then I am more than happy to continue to channel, as it is for the highest good.

Expansion

Chapter 4

What do I mean by expansion? There's many different views I guess, but I am offering you the spiritual understanding of expansion. Let me give you an idea with regards to Rahanni; when a student is attuned their aura expands by a further 3 feet, no matter how far the aura reaches out before the attunement. Once connected to 5th dimensional healing, this gives the student the opportunity to expand their consciousness that will vibrate out into the aura. This allows healing to take place, just by a friend or family member being in the Practitioners presence. This beautiful healing Light will flow through the Practitioner and be able to reach others no matter where they are, it is so beautifully done; so natural.

Just a few days after the attunement to Rahanni has taken place, the 'new' Practitioner will feel changes taking place, especially within the mind. He/she will begin to feel different about their life, they will start to question many situations they find themselves in right now and because the heart centre is also expanding, they will find the compassion held in their heart becomes stronger.

Members of their family feel changes going on, or maybe people at work see a different you. It does become quite noticeable and as weeks and months go by you realise others around you are changing also. They have absorbed positive Light from your expanded heart centre and this has an amazing knock on effect to all who come close to you.

Let me offer some ways of how you can make these positive changes in your life, by 'Creating through Joy'.

Going back to our previous ways of thinking, with regards to manifesting what we feel we want for the future; we have always understood that we view in our mind's eye the career, house, person etc; that we want in our life and with visualisation we could possibly create this 'dream' helping it to become reality at the appropriate time. Many people still hold on to this concept and that is fine, if that is what feels right for you, but I am about to show you another way of creating your 'dreams' now.

This is not rushing anything, it is gift from God/Source for this 'new' Golden Age, and has only been made available because of the planet raising its vibration, and Lightworkers/Star Beings have the ability to touch 5th dimensional vibrations. The 5th dimension is all about instant creation, for at this level no negativity can remain, as this dimension is geared to higher vibrations of spiritual Light, therefore negative energies cannot survive or become manifest. So connecting to the 5th dimension we rise above the heavier dense energy, allowing higher vibrations to manifest quicker without being held back by negative thoughts.

How many times have we said 'There must be something I can do to find out my mission here on Earth' or 'I am not sure what to do, should I go down this path; I can't sit and do nothing, I must plan ahead to get enough money to create my dream. I must work hard at this positive way of thinking and creating' No, you do not! We are just adding pressure to our self to bring abundance into our life; we become frustrated and think our guides and angels are not listening to our call. But they knew this was the old 3rd dimensional way of thinking, all has now changed, and we are a 4th dimensional planet with the ability to touch 5th dimensional vibrations.

We can create anything now with joy in our heart, without the concerns of where the money will come from to manifest that dream. This is all born out of fear, anger and feeling of lack in our life, all 3rd dimensional ways of thinking – this needs to change, it will take time of course to get used to the new way, but that word TRUST is all you need and the dream and desire to create for the highest good, for your soul and for your mission will be activated, especially when you do not force or rush your spiritual intentions.

Your new way of thinking is with joy in your heart, a feeling of being as one with universal energies, nature and who you truly are. This is the essence of spiritual growth in the 4th/5th dimension. Listen to the voice within guiding you, this is your I Am Presence guiding you towards your beautiful connection to God/Source. 'Work' no longer serves your higher purpose, it is all about 'feeling' 'being' and 'doing' that makes your heart sing that will create your dreams.

When you stop putting expectations on your desires you will be in alignment with 5th dimensional vibrations that can create abundance with thought and love combined. The right people will enter your life, the appropriate situation will be shown to you. It won't take any longer thinking this way than it does when you worry about work, money and feeling empty inside because of lack in your life. This old way of thinking holds back creation.

You will appreciate the joy of being healthy, having material things in your life won't be a necessity, it will come as a gift, if this is what is meant to be. You do not have to be without a lovely home, a car, a happy family life – all this is yours whenever you want it because the positive thoughts you hold in your heart with joy will be creating for you. Love heals and Love creates. Love your present situation, no matter how dire it may seem right now, for it is the gift of learning, showing you that change of thought can bring abundance into your life. You will be given many opportunities for these changes to take place. It is up to you as an individual to make it happen. No more relying on others to bring things, situations or people into your life – you can create with acceptance of joy and love in your heart. This is where you manifest your dream by being in the moment, relaxed, joyful and free from worry and expectations. This the 'magic' in your life, it is here right now, you don't have to wait, for 5th dimensional instant dreams. They maybe small to begin, but the more you trust, love and are joyful you can create. When you get used to thinking with joy during your day, you will find you receive a better quality of sleep at night, for the fears of the day are released and consequently do not manifest as 'bad' dreams at night.

Although we can manifest dreams quicker thinking with joy and love, what is brought to you may not be what you feel you want, but believe me, it will be for your highest good and the beginning of the transformation in your life. When you accept and appreciate the smaller gifts in life the larger gifts manifest also.

Take your time, do not rush anything and smile daily, thanking your guides and angels for the life you have right now and the beauty of nature that surrounds you. A smile raises your vibration, this in turn touches your heart centre and shines out into your aura, helping to manifest those dreams. It sounds simple, and it is. For I know, I have been down the road of the old ways of thinking and being and I know when I am happiest, because I have created more than I ever thought possible with a positive mind and the trust of my guides and angels.

Guides Galore!

Chapter 5

As Rahanni progressed over the years, it has become more powerful and has shown to open many heart centres within humanity, helping people to have a better quality of life, by releasing the negativity and fear based ways of thinking to that of a more positive, healthier and happier person.

The Ascended Masters, Archangels and Guides have stepped forward once again and have begun to make themselves known to all who wish to bring healing Love and Light to this world. They are offering their service, for they know little time is left on this planet for humanity to have a change in consciousness. To say this is urgent is an understatement, for still so much dark exists on this beautiful planet. We all need to take responsibility for humanities miscreation's and make sure we understand that just a few negative words from each of us, or judgements, adds to the dark vibrations on this Earth. We must control our thoughts and pause before we make a judgement or a statement of blame. It is easy to blame others for what is going on, but collectively we do add to these lower vibrations. It just takes a little more thought on our part. This is where our 'new' guides step in they are aware of a need for a change in consciousness and have decided to bring their positive Light into Rahanni to help, not just Practitioners but their clients also.

These beautiful guides recognise the importance of the 5th dimensional healing energy of Rahanni and have offered to channel through more of the God essence into each and every one of us, so we can eventually connect and help transform people's lives.

Let me introduce you to some of the 'new' members of our team and of the Spiritual Hierarchy who will work along-side all Rahanni Practitioners/Teachers. First we have Dr. Lorphan [pronounced Lorpan]; he is the Director of the Healing Academy on Sirius and held in the highest esteem by all of the Hierarchy for the dedication he shows to all healers on this planet and beyond. He is quite short in stature, features of the Orient, with a small 'goaty' beard, with an authoritarian presence: I am sure he will forgive my some-what earthly description, but it takes nothing away from the Love and Light held within every aspect of his being; this you can feel when he draws close to you, especially when teaching. With so much responsibility, this great being of Light expects respect, but he is also known to have a sense of humour.

Dr. Lorphan's connection with Rahanni is, amongst other things during the attunement procedure, where his vibration and love can touch your heart a thousand fold. He has a way of helping the student to feel so special at that moment in time and it has created many different experiences for all who become attuned; it is so beautifully done. There isn't an aspect of healing he cannot guide you on and he is available for all at all times, helping you with your own spiritual development.

Let me give you an idea of how he can work with you. I have taken some comments from the Rahanni manual that are presented to students, this will offer you some understanding of how we teach Rahanni.

Doctor Lorphan and his group of Galactic Healers are from the

connection.

We now come to another 'new' guide that wishes to work along-side, this is Phylos, a Tibetan Master of Joy. Phylos decided to connect with me a few years ago but will also work with all Rahanni Practitioners and Teachers. I am always amazed when I channel these beautiful 'beings' of Light and Love for I haven't a clue how they will interact at the beginning of our connection.

It was quite funny how Phylos was introduced to me because it came through a friend and one of my Teachers. I had an email from Kerry saying she had come across a book called 'Earth Changes' Teachings by Phylos. She didn't know why she was drawn to him or even how she stumbled across him, but intuitively was told to pass this information on to me.
I decided to do a meditation and to see if I could connect to Phylos. I didn't have to wait too long before I felt vibrations in my room changing, I had tingling over my body and felt my hair being touched; all classic signs of a connection. I remember calling out to Phylos and before I knew it I was having a lovely discussion, this is how we communicated.

Q. Are you Phylos?

A. 'Yes indeed'

Q Why was Kerry your first connection to me?

A 'You wouldn't have believed if I had just come and sat beside you saying, I am Phylos, we are old friends, your head was so busy you wouldn't have trusted. Your friend is an Angel of Light and receives much joy from helping others, and she would have been delighted to act as 'go between' as you say.

As the connection is so strong between you, I chose her light to wake you up. I knew she could do it, and she did very well, did she not?'

Q Why did you choose to work with me?

A 'You need all the help you can get bringing forth this healing Light known as Rahanni. You feel at times very alone, but trust me dear one, I am along-side for the duration. I am the one helping you to have the strength to come out of your comfort zone. It hasn't been easy I know, but as you are so dedicated to this mission I have to find a way of releasing your fears.'

Q I feel you have a sense of humour, am I right?

A ' Most certainly, every day you need laughter in your life, it raises your vibration and clears the cobwebs, so to speak. Just because I am of spirit does not mean I have to be sombre. This is not how God created me, or any of us. Laughter and smiles are a tonic, they bring so much healing into one's life – do they not? Every day I will find something to make you smile little one.'

Q Could you please tell me where you come from?

A 'I have had many lifetimes, most recent was in Tibet, I was a Doctor, you might say of Philosophy, Physics and Natural Law. Not your bag really is it? [I sensed his laughter, he knows me so well and my limitations.]'I am happy you wish to read my books, just take from them what feels comfortable and let the rest go, not your understanding yet.'

Q How are your energies compatible with mine when you are so learned and I am not?

A 'Stop putting yourself down little one, you have so much to offer. I adjust my vibration and connect to your personality. Your heart centre is indeed open and the stars flow from your heart reaching out across the globe to all of humanity. Your Light shines so bright, it is nearly blinding, but so full of God's love. Many people draw close to you, do you not feel them wanting to be a part of your Light? Yes, your Rahanni enhances your Light, but you have a natural ability; it is quite endearing.'

Q Have we met before?

A. 'Do you feel we have?'

Q Yes I do, but not sure where or when.

A 'I will tell you, many eons ago you tended my animals with Master Kuthumi when he was Saint Francis of Assisi. I had an animal, a donkey who was very sick, you healed him with your love and Light. Now – Have you not always had a love and a passion for Donkeys in this life time?' Phylos was laughing again. He is so right, I have always wanted a Donkey Sanctuary. He continued. 'That is your memory taking you back to the healing and our meeting. We never lose touch with the people and situations that are important in life and for our growth. Do you see now, are things beginning to make sense, and do not forget Tibet and your journey there.' [A story for another time.]

Phylos could sense I was tired and decided to bring this first communication to a close, stating that we would have regular connections, especially during meditations.

33

I feel truly blessed to say the least and I do hope you feel that something so very special has been offered to Rahanni Practitioners and Teachers, but even if those of you reading this book are not yet attuned to Rahanni, I am sure Phylos would love to connect in his own loving way.

The Book: 'Earth Changes' Teachings by Phylos.

ISBN. 1-4196-0301-9

Another healing connection is that of Helios and Vesta, a Copper/Gold ray of Light that was offered to me to help with the healing of Rahanni, healing on a deeper level. Helios and Vesta are from the Great Central Sun. not our physical sun, but suns beyond suns within the universe and the closest connection to God/Source. I was told this beautiful vibration of healing Light will help repair damaged cells and therefore can be used for healing of a physical nature. Copper as we know helps people with arthritic conditions, you often see people wearing copper bracelets, but we also have a combination of Copper/ Gold. This represents healing at amazing level. First the copper can reduce the inflammation and the Gold represents healing with White Light but with a sprinkling of Gold – in other words, Christ Consciousness. Now, whenever something new arrives to do with Rahanni I have to personally go through certain situations myself to prove, I guess how these new introductions can possibly work; this is no exception.

In 2010 approximately, I was diagnosed with Osteoporosis, and the Consultant offered me a Dexa Scan, this defines the strength or density of your bones. They scan the Lumbar spine, hips and upper femur. This gives a 'T' Score reading and if this reading is close to 3 you are diagnosed with Osteoporosis. My reading was 2.95 and the Consultant stated my bones were so thin that I could sneeze and crack a rib. He said I needed a particular medication, but I knew I couldn't have this, for one of the possible side-effects could be a thrombosis and I had already had one, albeit 30 years ago, but I wasn't prepared to risk it. So he said, he didn't know what else to offer me, except to do weight bearing exercises and eat green leafy vegetables. So I said, don't worry I will do healing on myself. He of course laughed and said 'Oh, you are going to do that Reiki thing I suppose' So condescending, I replied, 'No actually I am not, I will be using Rahanni, and yes, I know you haven't heard of it, but please write this in my notes'. He reluctantly did and said to go back and see him in a year. So I thought, right, let me try with Helios and Vesta, as this vibration should help to repair damaged cells, as this is what I was told by my guides. So for the next year, just 3 times a week for 7 minutes each time I began healing myself. I wasn't sure at what level it would work, but I trusted, but having no regard to the outcome. I went back a year later, they scanned the same areas as before and when I went in to see the Consultant, he said, 'I think you had better sit down' I was concerned, was my Osteoporosis worse, but to my amazement he said. 'You haven't got Osteoporosis anymore and in 30 years of doing this work I have never seen anyone's condition change like yours, I would like to say it was the medication I gave you, but I didn't give you anything, - what is it you do again?' Well, to say I was gobsmacked is an understatement, I asked what my 'T' Score reading was this time, he quoted, my Lumbar was 2, my hips 1.8 and my upper femur 2.2 that he said was the bones of a 25 year old. Oh my, I knew in my heart there would be changes in my condition but never as radical as this. I then said, 'I know you are of a scientific mind, but surely you can do something about this, as so many people are suffering' He just looked at me and said, 'If I took this to the board they would knock me down in flames, so no I can't take this any further.' I knew then that it was a waste of time trying to convince him to take further action, and without me stating the obvious, I guess you can see what I am trying to say.….. I leave that thought with you. All about revenue!

Now I am not writing this to say everyone who has Osteoporosis will be cured with Rahanni, all I am trying to say is, there's other ways to deal with many imbalances within our body, and we just need to be open to trying other avenues. Rahanni isn't a miracle cure but it does offer a better quality of life – I was lucky that Helios and Vesta was the appropriate healing for me, this doesn't mean to say everyone will get the same result, it may well be another therapy is right for someone else, but if we don't try, we won't know.

Many other guides are coming forward now to work with Rahanni Practitioners and Teachers and this is but a few I have mentioned. I feel so humble that these beautiful higher beings of Light are so happy to work along-side us at this most difficult time in our existence. I feel truly blessed that they trust me to bring this beautiful healing Light to all of humanity, it is such a joy.

Mother Mary Touches My Heart

Chapter 6

I cannot begin to tell you the excitement I felt the day Mother Mary appeared to me; my heart was fit to bursting with the love I could feel emanating from her heart to mine; this beautiful essence of Divine Light and Love. I had been sitting quietly in my healing room mulling over whether I should return to the recording studio to create a further meditation CD. This I have previously done with great success, as the testimonials I receive confirm this. It isn't something I do easily as I am quite a shy person and being centre of attention is alien to me, but I have been told on many occasions by my guides to come out of my comfort zone, so I listen to them, of course. I have now completed 4 CDs and it seems as though they have helped many people in different ways. I have received emails from many countries from people I will never meet because of distance, but I have managed to touch people's hearts and minds in a way that is appropriate for each one. For this, I am truly grateful to my guides offering me the opportunity to reach out to those in distress. Sorry, I digress! Back to my healing room. As I continued to sit quietly being overwhelmed by this beautiful vibration of loving Light a warm glow engulfed me and touched every aspect of my being. The tears began to flow when I heard a voice so soft and gentle. 'Carol, close your eyes and take your thoughts to your Ajna centre [3rd eye] whatever you see here I want you to draw'. Whoever was speaking to me sensed my confusion and began to speak. 'Please let me explain, I am Mary Anna, Mother of Jeshua Ben Joseph and I come close to you today for we, Jeshua and I require your help. We wish to reach out to humanity on a different level of healing, which is of healing the inner child. The healing you have offered with the beautiful vibration known as Rahanni has helped to open many heart centres and this is where we can move forward to heal the inner child. Many humans are still holding on to fear from the past, either from this lifetime or a previous life. They have not yet dealt with releasing all of the pain or hurt from these times, therefore it is blocking them from moving forward on their spiritual journey'. Listening to these beautiful words coming from Mary Anna, just left me speechless, I could not believe another gift was being presented to me, I felt truly humbled that again I was being trusted by these beautiful Higher Beings of Light and Love. Mary Anna continued to speak. 'As I offer you a symbol to be used for the healing of the inner child, it may seem simple, but that is intentional, this will allow all who use this to remember clearly how to mentally draw this over the client, or yourself of course, if healing this aspect of self is appropriate. This symbol will help to clear childhood memories that could have been painful in this lifetime or as I said before previous lives. Please use this symbol now in all of your healings either on its own or during your Rahanni healing sessions. This can also be visualised for Distant Healing also and remember, it may look simple but do not under-estimate the power of this symbol. Please include this is your paperwork when teaching and explain the importance of this symbol to your students. Every time this symbol is used for healing of the inner child an aspect of my Light will step forward with that of my son Jeshua [Jesus]. As you can see it shows the connection to us both, the M and the J written in Gold is a vibration from the God Essence for all who is in need. Please treat this with respect at all times, as this is the first time we have dedicated a symbol for healing combining both of our vibrations, this is the gift we offer you and humanity. This has only been possible because of the 5th dimensional energy of Rahanni and the raising of the vibration of the planet from the 3rd dimension to the 4th dimension – this allows all of the spiritual hierarchy to bring more gifts to humanity at this most difficult time in your existence. Use it well and with our Love and Light.

The healing of the inner child will help everyone to progress spiritually and to open their heart centres to more kindness, love and compassion. I wish to bring your attention back to the symbol Carol, for as you draw the sign you will notice a circle with a blue background and clouds rolling by, also Golden Sparkles of Light. As you visualise the symbol and you are looking through the window [circle] see those clouds go by taking the client/self, back to the time of pain or hurt in this lifetime or previous lives, the symbol in Gold will remain at all times when healing and just know that both Jeshua and myself have stepped forward and will be activating the clearing of the negative vibrations, then filling the void with the Golden Sparkles or as we know them, Adamantine Particles of Love and Light. This will create the deeper healing. Of course you can begin with the Violet Flame, as this transmutes negative energy, but to heal the inner child you need to work deeper and from a different perspective, hence this symbol. I am sure you will make this clear to all those you teach. More information is of course offered during the teaching of Rahanni, but this we hand back to you dear one. Thank you for accepting this precious gift and we know it will help create a deeper healing for humanity. Our Love and Blessings are forever with you. I am Mary Anna, Mother of Jeshua Ben Joseph.'

I am still in awe of the beautiful gift from Mother Mary and Jeshua, but I know in my heart the importance of the healing of the inner child, so humanity can release the old and move forward with love in their hearts and a change in consciousness. I would like to offer a deeper understanding of Mother Mary and her amazing journey and the importance of her life. Just take on board only that which resonates with your heart and let the rest go, maybe at a later date all will become clear. My truths are not necessarily your truths but I will share with you my understanding, but of course it is important that you are very discerning about what and who you allow into your life. Spirituality is a very personal experience, no two journeys are the same, for we have different needs and understandings at different times, but all I ask is that you are open to the information I am about to offer.

We hear or read in ancient texts the name 'Mary' so many times and we wonder why so many women are given this name. The name 'Mary' represents 'Matriarch' – Mother figure but was also given to those females who had raised their spiritual vibration to such a high level that it was a name of status within the spiritual hierarchy. The same also applies to the name of 'Joseph' the masculine vibration that was also of a higher spiritual level, again this was offered as a gift of status.

Mother Mary = Mary Anna her given name, a quiet being of calm authority but with a great sense of dedication to the Light. [Light with a capital 'L' represents the Light from God/Source, whereas light with a small 'l' is the light shining from the stars and universal light.] Mother Mary was an initiate of the Egyptian Mystery Schools and achieved a very high level of spiritual understanding and empowerment, this of course was required for her journey here on this planet.

Having a spiritual connection with Mary Anna [Mother Mary] and Jeshua [Jesus] is a joy to behold and a tremendously humbling experience for me, I will be forever their servant whilst I am still here on this earth plane and beyond. As soon as they draw close you cannot help but feel the warm glow of their devotion and love, it touches not just my heart but my soul. This experience is not just for the few but available for all of humanity. All that is required is to trust and open your heart centre to the spiritual gifts that can be offered from the Spiritual Hierarchy. As White Eagle once said, 'Much is given, but much is expected' in other words they offer spiritual gifts but we have to earn them, but all that is required is for us to be kind, caring, compassionate and coming from a loving heart. Not as difficult as some may think.

The Importance of the Violet Flame

Chapter 7

Before I move on, I know I have to mention the power, need and importance of the Violet Flame and its use on a daily basis. Some of you may be aware of this beautiful clearing/ transmuting and healing vibrational Light, but let me offer you a little understanding of the history of the Violet Flame.

People who have a spiritual understanding are possibly aware of this Divine Light, but I will share with you the information that has been offered to me from the higher beings, and the reason it is important for every human not just those attuned to healing modalities. Way back in the time of Atlantis, this was a place of hope, inner peace, love and compassion and every person was working for the good and benefit of each other, sharing so many aspects of life with the love held in their hearts. The Atlantic Ocean was its base and home to many advanced beings that understood technology way beyond anything we know now. The Violet Flame was available to all to help release any lower vibration that may be attached to them at some point. Although we have been told, through history, that the Atlantians were a loving race of people, but they still had a few issues at times, recognising these setbacks they would call on the Violet Flame to transmute any negativity releasing any fear, ego or insecurities, and this worked extremely well until the dark managed to get hold of this Violet Flame and used it for all the wrong reasons, therefore over a period of time this began to create havoc, and possibly the downfall of Atlantis. God/Source in his wisdom, decided to remove the Violet Flame from the planet until it could be used for all the right reasons.

In 1987 the time of the Harmonic Convergence an amazing amount of Lightworkers here on Earth began to send out love and healing Light across the planet, helping humanity to open their heart centres to more compassion. Saint Germain knew of the changes that would be taking place on Earth because of the shift from the 3rd dimension to the 4th dimension, a massive change in vibrations on this planet and knowing these changes would be very challenging, asked for a special dispensation from God/Source for the return of the Violet Flame, this was granted and in 1988 the Violet Flame was returned.

We understand the polarities of Light and Dark and we may think that God/Source should remove all the darkness from this planet, but majority of the dark energy has been caused by humanities miscreation's over millions of years and lifetimes. In a way we need to think of the dark as being useful, for recognition of these lower vibrations helps us to understand the difference between the two polarities and the need for transcending the lower vibrations. The dark is in fact our teacher, for we go through many experiences in all of our lifetimes, hopefully learning from each one. Life is about learning and understanding the difference between Light and Dark, for our soul needs to experience all types of vibrations to fully understand that we can create our own reality. If there is something happening in our life that is negative, then we need to make the changes to offer our self a better quality of life by releasing and letting go, this creates space for something or someone new to come into our life. We control our life, no one else. The guides cannot interfere for they know we have free will, but if you require help to move forward then you must ask the guides, that is universal law. As soon as you ask the relevant

43

guide or angel will step forward.

I digress slightly, but getting back to the Violet Flame and its importance; with the help of Saint Germain we are all now able to connect with the Violet Flame on a daily basis, by making a point of visualising or mentally placing a Violet Flame around your body, helping to release all negativity and fear based ways of thinking to that of positivity, love and compassion. Remember also to Violet Flame your home, for you would not want to add other people's negativity to your home when they visit. Yes you can use incense sticks, white sage or anything you feel releases lower vibrations, but I would always add the Violet Flame for I know personally how deep this can work.

So just to recap; the Violet Flame is available for all of humanity, not just the few. It is a tool for us to use daily, a gift from God/ Source to help us help our self. Anything that no longer serves our higher purpose, we can now release out into the ether, never to return. Rahanni Practitioner and Teachers are so aware of the Violet Flame for this is one of the most important parts of the teaching.

For more in-depth information you can find many books on the market of how to use this beautiful clearing vibration of healing Light.

Rahanni and Ascension

Chapter 8

Many people around the world are now aware of the beautiful healing Light of Rahanni Celestial Healing [a.k.a. Rahanni] it is at this moment being practiced in 24 countries and oh how it makes my heart sing when I hear of another country taking Rahanni to their heart. The emails or testimonials I receive on a daily basis just takes my breath away and makes me smile, for I know how Rahanni makes a difference to people's lives. Like anything, you need to go through situations yourself to understand how a healing modality really works, and believe me, I have been there and done that and come out the other side with the help of this beautiful healing Light.

Being the Founder of Rahanni I cannot just tell people how to use this healing vibration without having the experiences myself, and have I gone through challenges, all for the highest good of course. So I have personal experience of Rahanni with regards to the in depth healing it offers, but there is another connection to Rahanni and that is of humanities ascension process and how the two work hand in hand.

Anyone can be attuned to Rahanni as long as it resonates with their heart centre and they feel inside the need to offer help and healing to humanity, offering people a better quality of life, but an amazing chance to heal this planet.

When Rahanni was offered to me as a gift for humanity back in 2002, it was an amazing responsibility and I felt quite overwhelmed, although so humbled by the experience and to know how much the guides and angels had put their trust in me, but it was still daunting and maybe I became over protective for I remember thinking, who would be ready for a 5th dimensional healing energy, and who do I teach, maybe some people are not ready and the attunement would be too much for them. Oh my, so many questions. I didn't want to sit in judgement on anyone, but I knew Rahanni wasn't for everyone right now – so who do I teach? My lovely guide Kira stepped forward and told me not to worry as it wasn't down to me to decide who would be taught. If the guides felt it was too early for the student, then they would block them, until a later date. So the decision was taken out of my hands – what a relief! Kira told me the guides view the potential students Causal Body [more on this later] for this denotes how much Light is held within and how the student has progressed spiritually; showing that the student is ready to accept 5th dimensional vibrations, that of Rahanni. She also stated there may be times when I am teaching a student and possibly think, I do not understand why this person is here, for they hadn't been blocked by the guides. Kira stated, some students will benefit from the attunement alone without the need to go out and work as a healer. It is another way of helping people with their spiritual development. Luckily this situation doesn't crop up very often I am pleased to say, but now and again I have someone book an attunement day and I begin to think, 'why are you here?' but I get a nudge from the guides to say, 'leave this to us, for we know how that student will benefit – just be patient with them'. I just smile and think, 'you will have an amazing change in consciousness after this attunement'

What is Ascension? Every human will go through their ascension at some time in their existence, if not in this lifetime, it will be the next. Ascension is recognising heavy dense energies and transcending these lower vibrations. When a person begins to think 'there has to be more to life than this?' then the guides know they are ready to release and let go of the old negative ways of thinking and being and to progress and move forward on their spiritual journey. Ascension is raising your vibration from a lower energy to a higher vibration – a good analogy would be thinking of a radio station you are trying to tune into, a frequency of a higher and clearer level, so you can 'hear' better. Ascension will always be changing, on a personal and planetary level. When the planet shifts from one dimensional level to a higher level or vibration, it must have an effect on humanity, as we are all one, there is no separation. Everything that is living and breathing comes from one universal life energy and when one aspect changes it has a knock on effect to other connections on a planet especially when the energies are lighter, finer and move faster. How many times do we say, 'there isn't enough hours in the day for what I want to do', everything has speeded up. It isn't just older people feeling this, it is the younger generation also. This is the effect of the raising of the vibration of the planet, everything changes and it has a knock-on effect to humanity also. They begin their changes, their ways of thinking, a releasing of the old ways, needing to change career, move home, letting go of people that they no longer resonate with. This isn't out of judgement, it is to do with the ascension process, as I said earlier all of humanity will go through their ascension at some time in their existence, this you can be sure of. Our DNA is changing from a 2 strand to a 12 strand DNA. This is a massive change for humanity, the molecular structure of the mind and body will make great leaps in the future and again this is all part of the Divine plan for humanity.

Because of all the changes taking place, humanity will require help with these adjustments, this is where Rahanni comes into its own. It is, as I said a 5th dimensional healing that understands the changes required for the development of each and every person on this planet. The changes are subtle but need nurturing and healing, for as we go through these massive changes, our minds and bodies are playing catch up with these 'new' vibrations and will require help from those of us that have been through the changes already [and more to come] and can offer the help at a higher level of understanding. Humanity will be offered a better quality of life, working with communities, healing children and animals as we raise our spiritual vibration, and at last we begin to love our self more, that is so important.

I am going to offer you a deeper understanding of what I call 'Happy Ascension' I hope it resonates with your heart, as it does mine.

Happy Ascension.

Could it really be anything else! For as humans raise their spiritual vibration, they would have reached a level of development where gone are the everyday niggles in life, the wishing for this and wanting that. People on the ascension path transcend these aspects of illusion here on Earth, for they have expanded the heart centre to such a degree that material possessions are no longer at the top of the agenda. Don't misunderstand, there is nothing wrong with having a beautiful home, car and money, for this is part of humanity's journey. It is more to do with how these things materialize in someone's life. Some people have no problem with pushing forward, no matter who is hurt in the process as long as they get what they want. But if you have worked hard all of your life, you have helped others less fortunate and been there for people in distress, then beautiful gifts are offered, sometimes as a shift up the career ladder, meaning more money for you to share with your family. But the gifts that are truly magnificent are the spiritual gifts offered by the guides and higher beings of Light. Maybe the gift of spiritual realisation and an opportunity to see angels, archangels and higher beings of Light, even hearing their sound, their connection and expansion of the 3rd eye and the intuition. These are but a few of the gifts offered to humanity when the heart centre is expanded.

When people let go of all materialistic wants, a feeling of inner peace sits beautifully within the heart – for you feel and know you have all that you need. Good health, a loving family, enough money to feed and clothe your family, everything else that comes your way is a bonus and quite acceptable.

People often ask, 'What does it feel like to have no fear or worries in your life, as it seems an everyday occurrence for most people.' I always say to people, think of a time when you have been out in nature on a summer's day, the sun is beaming down warming your body, there is a gentle breeze that touches your face and you can see a beautiful landscape in front of you, with trees swaying in the breeze, or you sit under a tree for a short time and you become immersed in this idyllic picture, you become at one [at-one-ment] with nature you feel a part of all that is before you, free from worries or concerns. You have become the higher aspect of your soul, this feeling of bliss and inner peace is your soul touching your physical body and mind, offering you the experience that is yours forever as long as you wish. Whenever there is pressure in your life, just take yourself back to this moment in time, be at one with the essence of who you truly are, for everything else is but an illusion. There is no feeling quite like this on Earth, you are feeling and viewing all that you are and ever have been and ever will be; for this is Heaven on Earth and you can create this. Embrace this feeling daily, feel the quiet mind, the inner peace and the love held in your heart, for this beautiful creation has been gifted to humanity for as long as you want to embrace the essence of your soul's creation.

To have these feelings, all you need is to be kind, caring and compassionate, not just to others but yourself. Release and let go of all that no longer serves you in this lifetime and try to show others the way of having a 'Happy Ascension' As the Master White Eagle states; 'The Master looks for humility in his disciples, he looks for the single soul, faithful and loving. If you hold these qualities and let them become part of your everyday life, you will be used in the appropriate way. Yes, you will be tested on occasions for this is what your soul understands and yearns for, trying different paths and experiences, but finding a way of dealing with challenges in a positive way by releasing the negative.'

White Eagle also says, 'Keep your eyes twinkling, never look back, never look down, always look up and aim for the highest star' You can touch the realm of harmony and perfection just TRUST!

To offer yourself as a brethren of the Light, be watchful and alert of false values, it is so easy to get trapped in a net of disharmony. Be true to yourself and to God/Source, creator of all that is and ever will be.

These beautiful words are spoken by White Eagle, to find out more about this beautiful Higher Being of Light and Love contact the White Eagle Lodge, New Lands, Brewells Lane, Liss, Hampshire U.K. GU33 7HY

Is There a Heaven or Life on Other Planets?

Chapter 9

With regards to the above title, all I can do is offer my personal experiences; that is all anyone can do for we are not privy to another soul's journey. As I introduce you to my experiences please try to keep an open mind, but remember, my truths are not necessarily your truths, so just take what resonates with you and let the rest go for a later date, for when you have progressed or expanded your spiritual understanding.

I became aware of life beyond this Earth plane not long after my dear Mum passed to spirit, back in 1979. Mum had struggled with cancer for 2 years and at that time I was bringing up 4 daughters, holding down a full-time job, therefore I didn't give myself time to grieve for my Mum, until 2 years after her passing, I was sitting in my lounge speaking to Barrie, my husband and I said, 'I think I will give my Mum a call and tell her about….' Barrie cut me short in mid-sentence and said, 'Mate, your Mum isn't here anymore' Oh! My goodness, it had finally kicked in, after 2 years I was now realising what had happened, Mum wasn't at the end of a phone, as she had always been before. I wasn't able to share any concerns with her or talk about my girls, it just hit me so hard, I began to sob for the first time in 2 years, and this was the beginning of the grieving. I cried for what seemed like weeks. I couldn't work and I wasn't functioning. All I could do was cry, releasing so much pent up emotions in one massive out-burst. I took myself off to bed eventually, Barrie had retired earlier as he had an early start next day. I had just got into my bed, pulled the covers over and still feeling quite anxious and low when all of a sudden I felt a presence at the side of the bed. It was my dear Mum, she took my hand and said 'Come with me' before I had anytime to collect my thoughts or say anything I was lifted up and out of my body. I could still see myself lying in bed with Barrie by my side, but Mum spoke again. ' You must stay with me holding my hand but let me show you where I have moved to, you have shed so many tears and this makes me sad, so I am going to let you see the beauty that surrounds me, and look in front of you now, what do you see?' Oh! My, it is so beautiful, I am walking along a cobbled lane with a picket fence either side, I see little white houses dotted about in the countryside, there's flowers that I have never seen before and I honestly couldn't describe for these colours do not exist on Earth. This place reminded me of a Greek Island, it was so peaceful and so beautiful, but as I looked closer at one of the houses, someone was looking out of the top window, smiling and waving, it was my dearest Dad. He had passed to spirit when I was 2 years old and he was the reason I was on a spiritual journey, for he had been a healer back in the 1940s. My heart skipped a beat and I wanted to run to him and hold him so close to me, but I wasn't allowed. Tears were streaming down my face but my heart was filled with so much love, I wanted to stay with Mum and Dad, I didn't want to go back, but Mum spoke quite firmly. 'You must go back sweetheart, you have too much to do, but you can now see how happy we are and we will wait for you when it is eventually your time to come home, but for now I will take you back to your life and I want no more tears.' The next thing I remember was my hand dropping on the mattress, I was back in bed, Mum had gone, but I was still full of so much love in my heart and to see my Mum and Dad so happy was such a joy and I knew all was well, I still had tears but this time tears of joy not sadness. I tapped Barrie on the shoulder and said, 'I have just

53

seen my Mum and Dad, it was so beautiful.' He replied, 'Great, tell me in the morning.' He thought I had had a vivid dream, but I knew it was my first out of body experience. What a journey, what a joy!

So, is there a Heaven? As far as I am concerned yes, I know with all of my heart this to be a truth and I have seen where the majority of us go when it is time to return home, the home of our soul, but I also know now so much more, and I will share with you details of other adventures I have had as we move forward through these pages. Be prepared for some new information, or maybe some different ways of thinking.

I will now move forward with another aspect of the soul's journey that we could possibly take, as I said earlier. Please have an open mind and try not to judge what you do not understand, as there will come a time when all is revealed, this is known as Divine Timing where the truth is unveiled and all is shown in its glory.

Many people who are still connected to the old 3rd dimensional way of thinking, believe it is a myth and there is no such thing as life beyond the Earth. Well sorry to quash that belief, but I am here to tell you, think again! There is life on many other planets within the universes – yes, plural, more than one universe, more than our human minds can comprehend right now. I will just touch on some of the journeys I have experienced, but remember, this is a journey of my soul, we are all different and you will have the journey that is appropriate for you whilst here on Earth.

Because Rahanni is a 5th dimensional healing, the vibration/energy is connected to 3 planets within the Milky Way, of which

Earth is a part of. The names of these planets are Andromeda, a Galaxy in its own right, but vast enough to touch the Milky way, Sirius – known as the dog star, but also the Great White Lodge, the spiritual home for Ascended Masters and Higher Beings of Light and Love. Then we have the Pleiades – a cluster of over 200 stars but only 7 are visible by the naked eye, this is known as the 'seven sisters'. These planets are home to many advanced civilisations and are spiritually and technologically more advanced in many ways. They also hold the most amazing vibrations of healing Light and this is where Rahanni originates from. Because of the gift of Rahanni presented to me and the knowledge required to offer healing and teaching, I was given the opportunity to visit or should I say touch the vibrations of these planets, so I could offer a deeper understanding to all of the students that felt drawn to this healing Light.

I was told the visit to these areas would be short but that I would be protected at all times, for a guide would take me on the journey of discovery and a journey of a lifetime. There was a need to have some understanding of the areas that Rahanni had been a part of, and as I would be describing these planets, it was good idea that I had some knowledge of them to relay back to students. The first journey was to Andromeda, the home of the sea creatures, dolphins and whales. I was amazed beyond belief of what I was about to view. I could see waterfalls of Turquoise, pink, silver and violet, dropping down on both sides into a lake or pool, I noticed little heads popping out of the water making the most joyous sound, it was of course the dolphins. Oh! What joy for me to view them in their natural surroundings, splash-ing in and out of the waterfalls, then the larger whales moved towards me, I under-estimated the size and power of these amazing creatures. Everywhere I looked, every sea creature you could think of was here and they emanated rainbow light. What a joy to behold, I would never forget this moment as dolphins had always held a place in my heart, and always would.

My time on Andromeda was over and I was to move on now to Sirius, such a vast place again with Temples everywhere, some with large Golden Domes, others smaller, but the vastness of this place is truly magnificent. This is home to the Great White Brotherhood, a place where ascended Masters go to meet and discuss how they can help planets within the universe that are having difficulties or to work with them to help raise their vibration. I was told to stand back and just view silently. I noticed in a particular area a marble table that was half-moon shaped with chairs around the edge and one chair opposite. This was occupied by a very High Being of Light, his name was Sanat Kumara, he is the Earth's Planetary Logos, he presides over the initiation and ascension process of every human on this planet; you may have heard of him during your spiritual teachings. I was told to view the left hand side of the temple and as I gazed upwards I noticed a doorway, although it seemed hazy, but I was told this is a portal that has opened to allow the Higher Beings through that were about to take their place around the table for discussion. I could not believe what I was seeing, I noticed Melchizedek the Universal Logos, flow through, then Master Kuthumi, Chohan of the 2nd ray and world teacher, Kwan Yin, Mother of Compassion, Lady Nada, Ascended Master of the 6th ray of Devotion. So it went on, all of these Higher Beings of Light taking their place at the marble table, ready for their discussion. Time for me to leave, so I was told. Such an amazing insight into how these Higher Beings of Light and Love come together to help all planets at all times. What a gift for me to be a part of this momentous occasion, even though my stay was short.

Off I go, this time to The Pleiades, a place that is familiar to me, but I do not know why, until I was told, this was my planet of origin. When a soul is first breathed into existence, it has to begin its journey on a planet somewhere within the universe, this was evidently mine, The Pleiades, a planet of love of nature and music. This planet is helping humanity right now with the growing of foods without pesticides and to grow organically, they are helping people have a change in consciousness with regards to this matter of maybe having an allotment to grow vegetables, or to take half of your garden and use it for cultivating food, but still have shrubs, flowers etc. it's about finding a balance between the two. The Pleiadians have a love of music and I could hear soft angelic tones flowing all around me and it so touched my heart, as I also love music, but I guess this is the connection to my planet of origin. I was told many of the Pleiadians are taking on physical form right now to help humanity develop their understanding of nature and the importance of the bees and butterflies for helping with pollination. We still seem very naïve about this important subject, but with the help of the Pleiadians we will know in our heart just how to offer our understanding and spread the word to others, before it is too late.

Understanding the Soul.

Chapter 10

So many people have asked, 'What is the soul and where does it come from?' I will offer my understanding, but please just take on board the information that resonates with you and within your heart, let the rest go. All will be revealed when you return home.

As we progress with our spirituality we do recognise the physical body is a vehicle for the soul to use when experiencing many journeys within the world of matter and form. I now wish to add to this information stating the original vibration of the soul is and was a star from the universes before it was offered a physical body. This information may shock some of you and maybe you will have difficulty getting your head around this concept – for all of your previous beliefs and understanding was that God/Source created man in his own image. Yes this is true, but not in the way we have previously been told; there is more, as you will find out as you continue to read.

Before we were breathed into existence as a human being, we were star energy – a beautiful vibration of light that resonates from the heart of the Divine, God/Source. These star vibrations were the breath of God/Source. When the time was right, a star was created by the outbreath of the creator, bringing forward light into the universes. The largest and brightest light was that of Lord Metatron, creator of all the outer light within the universes.

Let us look at the creation of the soul from a different perspective. The monad is a Divine spark from God/Source. It is also known as the I Am Presence. It was the first core intelligence and individualised identity. It also had freedom of choice. This intelligence decided it wanted to experience a denser form of the universe than it was living in. So each of our monads with the power of its mind created 12 souls. Each soul is a partial representation of its creator, the monad. So God/Source created millions of monads and each monad created 12 individualised souls. Each soul then deciding to experience a denser form of the material universe created 12 soul extensions or personalities and that is us. So we on Earth are personalities or soul extensions of our soul. Just as our soul is an extension of a greater consciousness, our monad. Our monad is an even greater consciousness of God/Source the Mother and Father of all creation. Wow! Hope you got that! This wonderful information comes from Joshua David Stone, his many books are so inspiring.

The soul will always be growing and learning on the higher realms of existence and will only merge with the personality when the individual personality recognises and becomes more aware of its soul presence and understands spiritual matters from a higher perspective. The soul will then take more of an active role in helping the personality to raise its consciousness.

The physical, mental and emotional aspects are the garment of the soul. Remember, the soul is not perfect, it is always in the process of growth and development and all souls are at their own level, as no 2 souls are the same and never will be. They are separate vibrations, but connected to the other 11 soul extensions in their soul group. The 12 soul groups are striving towards a higher Christ/Universal consciousness. Even monads are not perfect they will continue to develop and evolve. All soul extensions/personalities help the others within their group to evolve; it is beautifully done!

The soul and monad will always guide us as personalities, we just have to learn to communicate with these higher aspects of self and TRUST! When we hear of 'old souls' these are the souls that have incarnated on earth-like planets that require form. The average soul with its 12 soul extensions could have up to 2,000 lifetimes, the 'old souls' has up to 3,000 lifetimes.

In the Alice Bailey books, she states that happiness, joy and bliss are different states of existence. Happiness is the personality reaction – Joy is the quality of the soul and Bliss is a quality of at-one-ment with the monad.

We have different aspects of the soul, Light and Dark. Some souls are confused and have chosen different paths to go down. Instead of travelling the path of service and unity of all in existence, this being the path of Light, many have chosen the path of the dark, seeing others as objects and not as fellow souls. They exploit others and use them for their own self-gratification, causing pain and suffering. They do not care about the hurt they cause as long as they get what they want. Unfortunately they are creating a karmic situation for them-selves at a later date in their existence, where the laws of karma will catch up with them. They will have to become accountable for their actions, but hopefully they will decide to recognise the Light of God/Source within their own 3 minds and 4 bodies and begin a journey of discovery within the light and release the dark. It is up to each individual soul extension to develop at its own rate, but it is amazing how rapidly one can grow with the opening of the heart centre, where the Light of Christ consciousness resides. Every minute of every day your own unique soul can grow and develop with an act of kindness and with the love you hold in every aspect of your being.

Knowing your Tone.

Chapter 11

We now understand a little more of the journey of the soul but I wish to add extra information for you. When our soul was breathed into existence a special and unique gift was given. This was a tone or sound that resonated with the God essence and this would remain with that soul forever. No two soul's tone or sound is the same, it is unique to each individual, the most incredible gift we could have ever received. It was a blessing from the 'Divine' stating that our soul will be forever part of the God essence, no matter how many journeys are made and how many Universes or Galaxies a soul travels to including the Earth.

The journeys that have been under-taken have always had, first the original tone/sound, but another tone is offered for each soul when it is created into form, whether it is on planet Earth or another planet in a different realm of existence. Because the incarnated soul will have to adjust to the vibrations of its next incarnation and to the vibration of the said planet. It will need to be compatible with its surroundings, no matter how obscure or unusual we may think in our human way.

So you may ask why we need these tones. I will try to keep things simple. Each journey our soul undertakes will be required to hold an essence of the place it has decided to move on to, growing and learning as before. It may be the soul wishes to travel to another planet, such as Venus to continue its spiritual journey, or possibly Sirius, where I must say, this is where many Lightworkers will eventually move to at some time in their existence, where they will connect to Dr. Lorphan, Director of the Healing Academy on Sirius and planet Earth. The soul in question will of course still hold its original tone/sound, but it will now be offered another tone/sound to help it integrate with all the vibrations of its chosen planet, therefore making it easier for the soul to move forward and learn and understand the teachings and qualities of this new planet. The soul will be drawn again to like-minded energies and will be shown how to integrate with other beings of Light. This of course will again be a unique tone/sound but will resonate with other souls of a like mind.

Scientists understand one aspect of this and they will possibly state it is one person's psyche connecting to another's psyche that is bringing them together, but it is more than that. It is the God essence blending with other individuals at the appropriate time to help bring about a possible healing, balance, inner peace, harmony, love, kindness and compassion. All traits from our first aspect of creation that originates from the 'breath of God'. A knowing or feeling so deep at our soul level.

You can always recognise a very 'old soul' – one who has had many journeys for they are the Lightworkers who have struggled over many years and lifetimes, having harder tasks and more intensive training.

Certain types of music may touch your heart as you feel it echo within every cell of your body. You could feel inner peace, calm and relaxed, other types may uplift you, offering to energise you, but then there is the heavy dense sound of maybe heavy metal music that doesn't normally sit very well or feel comfortable with most Lightworkers, and the vibration is too dark, making you feel uneasy or uncomfortable, definitely not for you!

You can see how we connect to sounds and rhythms, especially that of nature, trees, plants, birdsong or the sea. We have the feeling of relaxation when in these surroundings for this resonates with our hearts.

Everything in the universe is vibrating with energy and sometimes a sound may call us closer, especially to nature. Try to listen to the sounds when you next take a walk in nature or by the sea, for as these sounds touch your heart you are at one with the universal life force – the God essence. You can feel vibrations pulsing through your mind and body. This is our true self, our soul, having a gift so unique that it has the ability to connect to the sounds of the universe and beyond.

The Mahatma and its importance.

The word Mahatma means Great Soul/Being. This vibration has been connecting with humanity since 1987, the time of the Harmonic Convergence, when all Lightworkers sent out to the planet love and Light in abundance. The Mahatma is also our link between us as personalities and the Godhead/Source.

When we ask the Mahatma to connect, it radiates with 12 rays of light; we view this as the Golden White Light, but in truth it is so much more. As powerful as it is, it can flow through our being at every level, but our body is strong enough to hold this amazing vibration, because it is channelled through each person's monad and soul, making it useable for the incarnated personality.

There is no other energy that we can call on that is of a higher frequency and vibration. It is available for everyone, not just Lightworkers; healing the soul as well as other aspects of our 3 minds and 4 bodies. The benefit of calling the Mahatma is to help with our ascension process and the building of our Light Body, helping us to deal with our earthly lessons and experiences in a quicker and a more positive way.

When receiving the Mahatma, your body may feel it is heating up, this will be the energy pouring in, and as we continue to call the Mahatma and use it for our spiritual growth, ascension and to help others, information is reported back to the Higher Beings of Light, Ascended Masters and God/Source; therefore the continuation of our journey is adjusted daily, especially when we hold more Light. This Light we gain when we live our life with kindness, love and compassion and it is held within our Causal body. Cause and effect – what you give out you must become accountable for at the end of this journey. The more Light you hold in your Causal body will denote where your next journey will be, when we eventually return home.

We will not be allowed to anchor more of the Mahatma than our physical body can deal with, hence you cannot rush your spiritual growth, although some do try, but then they will be held at a level that is appropriate for them at that time. Get to know the Mahatma vibration, for as it flows through your body it has a way of releasing any viruses that may be around, helping to keep you free from these lower eneriges. MAHATMA = ALL 12 RAYS OF LIGHT – GOLD/WHITE.

An activation from Jeshua Ben Joseph [Jesus]
Channelled by Carol A Stacey

Chapter 13

As you read through this page, this will be an opportunity for you to receive and activation from Jeshua Ben Joseph [Jesus] It will be absorbed into your higher consciousness at the appropriate level, so please do not worry about accepting this, for your guides will allow this to be absorbed if it is the right time and for your highest good. If it isn't the correct time, then as you read through anything that is not acceptable will not be assimilated.

If you feel this is appropriate, you will be able to offer this to any group you may be connected to, go by your intuition.

'Welcome my children on this special occasion, a coming together of deeper vibrations within your heart centres. On this day of joy we will join our hearts together and send out Light and love across the planet, helping those who are feeling lost, abandoned or lonely at this most difficult time. We must not let them feel they are on their own, for we need to touch their hearts with the Divine Love and Light that is there for all of humanity. We can offer this by visualising a Golden Grid of Light surrounding this planet and with our thoughts from deep within our hearts we will shower the Golden Rays through each person's crown and through their central nervous system, helping it to flow through every aspect of their being.

First we must create a Violet net around this planet, be like a fisherman and cast your net way out in to the void and watch how it settles over the Earth, freeing humanity of the negative vibrations. Reel your net in, and again cast it out across the Earth, do this once again, 3 times in all, for each casting of the Violet net will help diminish the fear and negativity that is held within the aura of humanity. Sit quietly for a few moments and let the powerful and loving Saint Germain help the angels clear away the dross and debris. There is no need to focus on just one country, for all will be covered at the appropriate time.

Please do not worry about lack of visualisation for it is the intent that is more important.

As you sit quietly in the sanctuary of your own heart, just see this Light flowing through the Golden Grid, just like a shower, gently pouring over every country and every person, touching them with healing Light, helping to raise their consciousness to a higher level of understanding. Continue to visualise, then sit quietly again whilst the activation takes place within yourself.

You can offer this activation anytime, weekly would be ideal, for as you connect to your heart centre and use your visualisation/intent, just know you are contributing to the well-being of all of humanity. Just trust, for when you offer something to others with pure intent it will create a beautiful space filled with Love and Light.

Just let me speak to each one of you reading or hearing this right now, for we of the Spiritual Hierarchy know of your growth and of your spiritual development and we also know accepting this path is not always easy. You may feel at times you take 2 steps forward and then 3 steps back, but just know this my dear ones, we never leave you for a second. As your heart makes that beat it beats in rhythm with my heart and that of the Creator God and Protector of all life, for we are one. This I feel you understand but maybe you also feel that we, of the Hierarchy step back and let you continue your journey alone – we do not. We never leave you, all we ask is that you trust our love and devotion to you and we know of your trials and tribulations but we cannot take these away, for this is your soul's journey and that we do not interfere with in any way.

Bring into your heart that knowing of Divine Grace, Joy and infinite Love that is your pure and true essence. When you recognise who you truly are – a son or daughter of God then you understand that every parent wants their child to be happy and free from any negative ties that bind them to any dark vibration. Always see the Light in everything, even in your darkest hours, it will be there. It takes courage to see this but you have that courage, stay strong of heart and mind and know we are just a breath away, trying to brush the cobwebs from your mind and to help you search for the Light.

I will take my leave of you now as you continue to journey forward, absorbing more of the Golden Rays, use it daily dear ones and you will see the beauty of your existence and feel the joy in your hearts, knowing I am but a breath away.

Many Blessings to your heart from my heart; we are One!' I am Jeshua Ben Joseph.

I hope you have enjoyed this connection to Jeshua and feel you are able to help not just yourself but all of humanity from a different perspective and understanding.
Please share this activation when you come together within groups, as group

71

energy creates a higher vibration of Light and Love that will help to reach out across this planet.

The Light Continues to Shine

Chapter 14

I have tried to offer you an understanding of how Rahanni has moved forward since the healing gift was presented to me back in 2002 and to say it has been an amazing and wonderful journey is an under-statement. I have met some beautiful souls and many have become friends, this so touches my heart as we are all on a similar journey of discovery. First it is about finding our self, for being connected to spirit can be a lonely place, you are not sure who to talk to about the healing or how to get a message out to humanity, but with support this will help your confidence. With Rahanni many have found that support is always there, for we have a Facebook page, albeit a private page just for Rahanni Practitioners and Teachers that you will be invited to join. Having that support is crucial and I would find it difficult to call Rahanni an organisation for we are more than that, we are a Family of Love and Light. I will not have Rahanni accredited or known as an organisation for how can someone sit in their office and dictate to me how Rahanni should be run, many have tried and I will not conform to other people's expectations of what Rahanni should or shouldn't be. They have not been privy to my journey with Melchizedek and they know nothing of Rahanni in anyway, so who gives them the right to dictate and tell me how to run this beautiful healing modality. Sorry, I digress, but this is something I am quite passionate about.

It isn't just about a student being attuned to this beautiful healing Light and for me to tell them to go out there and heal as many people or animals as you can, it is more than that. The attunement of Rahanni is important for the individual, as it will help with spiritual development and growth and if this is all that happens that is fine with me, but if the student or now a 'new' Practitioner wishes to go out and offer healing to all of humanity, to me that is a bonus. I put an emphasis on the student becoming aligned with its soul and higher consciousness purely through having the attunement of Rahanni.

I have seen many changes in people after that special day of the attunement and they would be the first to admit how their life has changed. But it can also have a positive knock-on effect at home where possibly the partner or children in the Practitioner's family begin to change also. It cannot be anything other than positive, for when the attunement takes place, the aura of the student expands another 3 feet, no matter how far their aura stretched out before, therefore when they go home, the family begin to feel changes taking place, and then you find peace and harmony being created rather than anger and frustration, oh it is beautifully done.

I wish to share with you a personal situation with regards to my husband Barrie. A self-confessed non believer in spirituality, although very supportive in what I do, but does not want to get involved in any way. I have been communicating with guides and angels for so many years now that it is a regular situation for me, especially on a daily basis, and when I am writing or teaching, they all seem to draw close and offer me information for the highest good of all. I am so appreciative of all that they do for me and I did ask my guides if they could help Barrie open his heart centre a little more to a possible spiritual experience. Bearing in mind, if you have read my first book of how Rahanni came to me, you would know he did see Melchizedek in our bedroom on the night I was presented with the gift of Rahanni, but since then he hasn't wanted to know. So I thought, oh well, it isn't going to be his journey this time around and left it at that. Then one day I was at the hospital sitting in the waiting room waiting for a scan when Barrie said 'What does this mean?' he was holding his hands out and moving them backwards and forwards, up and down. I said. What do you mean, playing the piano?' He laughed, 'No, when you work with Rahanni'. 'Oh, you mean when I am healing, my hands hover over the client and they move up and down.' 'Yes', he replied. 'But have you got a monk as a guide?' Feeling confused, I said yes, but wondered why he had asked. 'Oh well, he must have been doing healing on you last night, I sat up in bed and watched him.' I couldn't believe what I was hearing, this non-believer had seen my guide offering healing to me and he was just so matter of fact about the whole thing. But that wasn't the end of the conversation, he evidently noticed 2 other 'beings' in our bedroom but forgot to mention it before. I couldn't stop laughing and said to Barrie. 'I thought you didn't want to know about spirituality, but you seem to see more than me.' He just turned and said, 'Well they are there for you not me and I keep telling them to go away but they don't seem to listen, so I thought, well if they want to turn up in the middle of the night, that's fine, as long as they don't keep me awake.'

So, you can see, the vibration I now hold in my aura, has had an effect on Barrie, helping him to become more aware of his spiritual side, but it will take more time for him to accept these visions; but that is his journey. I am not saying this will happen in every family, it is just to show you that we as Practitioners/ Teachers expand our aura, and it can have a positive effect on other people we meet. Please don't think this will happen to everyone at night, it rarely does, but be open to their messages of love, for this is what they are.

I am delighted Rahanni is now in 24 countries across the planet and it truly makes my heart sing when I get an email or phone call from a prospective student saying how they want to be a part of Rahanni. The Light Continues to Shine and this is what it is all about, touching the hearts of humanity offering a better quality of life. If this book has opened your eyes in some way then maybe Rahanni is for you, just go within and see if this beautiful healing Light resonates with your heart – I do hope so.

Love shines from my heart to all of the Rahanni Practitioners and Teachers that are spreading the word across the planet and I hold you all in the highest esteem for your trust in me and the trust of our wonderful guides and angels. Please feel free to contact me via my website: www.rahannicelestialhealing.co.uk

Love and Blessings

Carol A Stacey – Founder of Rahanni Celestial Healing. F.R.C.H./F.A.C.C.

Testimonials from Students and Clients.

Thank you Carol for the Rahanni attunement; it was a most beautiful and enlightening experience. I feel fine and just waiting for the energy to settle, but feeling very peaceful. I feel an underlining beautiful and yet powerful energy manifesting in my life that I can't wait to share with others. I am so pleased I heeded the calling to be attuned to Rahanni, this I know will be life changing. You are an amazing and wonderful woman and it is a privilege to work with you and Rahanni.

[New Practitioner David from Sussex]

Rahanni has made a big difference in my life to me and my family. I feel I am meant to Teach Rahanni and will be flying to the UK in the Spring, I hope you have some spaces left for me to be taught so I can help many people in the USA.

Meeting you has changed my life and I sing your praises from the rooftops and that of Rahanni. Much love and gratitude.

[Rahanni Practitioner] Lizzie.

I recently attended a Rahanni Practitioner training day with Trisha in New Zealand. [Flew in from Australia] It was simply one of the best days of my life. Trish is an amazing Teacher but thank you Carol from my very soul for bringing through the most beautiful gift of Rahanni. I feel my life has shifted to another level in a much more positive way.

Pauline [Practitioner] Australia.

I have received the most amazing healing and for once in my life I have stood up to someone who has been controlling, but I have taken back my power and after just 3 sessions I feel I have been reborn. I now know I can achieve anything, where before I had no self- esteem and lacked confidence that has all gone thanks to the beautiful healing with Rahanni.
[Debbie from Essex Client]

I had a Rahanni session with Louise and I would highly recommend her and the healing to anyone.

I felt a deep sense of healing taking place within my heart centre, I had a few tears, but realised this was a gentle clearing. Louise's approach is so gentle, positive and effective and I look forward to further sessions.
[Ali from Suffolk Client]

I have known Carol for many years and have recommended patients of mine to consult her mainly with stress related problems, often not responsive to conventional treatment. The results have been truly astonishing both in degree of improvement and rapidity. My confidence in Carol has increased over the years to the point where I feel able to almost guarantee to the patients a marked improvement in their condition.

We have worked in consultation and I regard Carol's role as one of a complementary practitioner rather than that of an alternative one. I would most strongly commend her to you and let the results speak for themselves.
[Dr. R Macdonald G.P. Essex]

I found Rahanni healing through a friend and as soon as I had a chat to Carol Stacey I knew this was just what I had been searching for. Rahanni healing changed my life from the moment of my attunement.

Rahanni opened my heart centre, raised my vibration but it has also helped to me look at life, humanity and the planet in a much more positive way. Rahanni gave me the confidence to become a teacher, passing my knowledge on to others. The only way I can describe how I feel is, before my attunement I was viewing a black and white TV but after the attunement I started to see much more colour, 9 years later the colour gets stronger every day.

I am so grateful to Carol for her hard work and dedication, bringing Rahanni healing to the Earth and in so many other countries. Carol totally comes from her heart centre with so much love always putting others before herself; Carol is a beacon of light for us all.

I feel so grateful every single day that Carol is my teacher and my beautiful friend.
[Margaret Mersea Island Essex. Teacher]

I really enjoyed my day with you and it was so fascinating to learn about Rahanni. Sometimes when I have read someone's book and been excited to meet the author, I have been disappointed, but not with you. As soon as I met you I felt your warmth and genuineness. As you spoke, spirit shone through your eyes and I could have spent days lapping up your knowledge.
[Moira from Essex Practitioner]

To read an amazing amount of testimonials please go to the website of Neshla Avey the Rahanni Teacher/Elect as Neshla will be taking Rahanni over from me when it is time for me to go home. www.neshlaavey.com A beautiful soul with an amazing open heart.

Closing Comments

I do hope this small book has opened your hearts and minds to further spiritual understanding.

I have offered you some personal information but purely to let you know, all that is presented to me by the higher beings of Light and love is for my growth and development, and as a teacher of spiritual concepts, I have to practice what I preach, so to speak, but to let you know about the many paths or journeys our soul travels down and that nothing is wasted. We learn from every situation, negative or positive, it is about balance, helping us to find a balance between the earthly life and our spiritual life.

Some added information that may help with your spiritual understanding; every New Moon and every Full Moon this planet is presented with 2 vibrations of light, that being the Magenta ray and the Turquoise ray. These rays are very important, for when a female absorbs the Magenta ray this offers strength of the feminine mind, helping women to stand up for their beliefs and take back their power. When the male absorbs the Magenta ray it goes directly to the heart centre, expanding this and helping them to become more compassionate. The Turquoise ray will have the same effect on both male and female, as it is absorbed into the mind and body it will help with healing of self and a change in consciousness. These 2 rays of light will continue to flow through our minds and bodies until 2028, when we should have absorbed enough of these rays to help with each person's ascension process that everyone will go through at some time in their existence.

Blessings and Namaste!

Carol A Stacey

1/24